Power Principles

12 Great Affirmations for Leaders

Michael H. Harbour II

ISBN: 9798668013319
ISBN-13: 979-8668013319

DEDICATION

This book is dedicated to two very special ladies in my life: Mammaw (my grandmother) and my wife, Constance.

Mammaw went to Heaven in 1998 but is always in my heart. Her words of encouragement still ring in my thoughts.

My wife, Constance, whom I love dearly, is the only lady who could have replaced the love of Mammaw.

I dedicate this, also, to my two gifts from God: William Clayton and Isabella Reece.

You are the light of my life and the reason I strive to grow as a leader every single day.

To all of you:

"I love thee to the depth and breadth and height my soul can reach." - Elizabeth Barrett Browning

CONTENTS

ACKNOWLEDGMENTS

This book would not be possible without the dedicated effort of my business manager, Brenda Dunagan. Brenda has spent hours helping me write, edit, and clarify my ideas in not only this project but many others yet to come.

I want to thank Dr. John C. Maxwell for offering me the opportunity to partner with him and the John Maxwell Team of International Coaches, Speakers, and Trainers.

There are too many to name on this team who have helped me along the way, but one in particular is Deb Ingino, CEO of Strength Leader Development. Deb is a leader of leaders and has encouraged my ideas and given me confidence in my ability like no one else.

And, finally, I thank all the leaders who have written, recorded their messages, and spoken their words. I have been mentored by hundreds who don't even know I exist; yet, without them living their calling, I would not be who I am today.

Most of all, I am grateful for the greatest leader ever, Jesus Christ, whose teaching has transformed my life in countless ways.

INTRODUCTION

What is an affirmation?

In essence, it is a statement of principle...a confirmation of what you see as truth. The pages that follow cover *12 Great Affirmations for Leaders* – time-tested principles to help leaders build strong foundations.

I trust you will take these principles to heart and be inspired to take action where needed – to become a leader fully ignited!

POWER REFLECTIONS: This page is provided for the leader in you to reflect on each affirmation and determine how you will apply it to your life and leadership.

_____

_____
_____
_____
_____
_____
_____
_____
_____
_____
_____
_____
_____
_____
_____
_____
_____
_____
_____
_____
_____
_____
_____
_____
_____
_____
_____
_____
_____
_____
_____

Affirmation #1 - Attitude

The people I lead reflect the attitude I model;
I will reflect an attitude that leads people
higher in purpose, excellence, and action.

*"Your attitude, not your aptitude,
will determine your altitude."*

- Zig Ziglar

A PILOT WITH A GOOD ATTITUDE

Let's imagine you are the pilot of a jet, flying thousands of feet in the air, with passengers onboard. It is critical that you maintain a good attitude.

Attitude, in aeronautical terms, is the indicator of the plane's ability to stay airborne. A plane is continually shifting due to outside forces of wind and gravity. Constant adjustments are needed to maintain the balance of pitch, roll, and yaw. This balance creates a proper attitude – one that will ensure you and your passengers safely reach your destination.

Perhaps your days are spent in an office instead of a cockpit or at the helm of a business instead of in the pilot's seat. Attitude is just as important to you as it is to a pilot. Those who follow you depend on you having a proper attitude. In life and business, as in flying, there will always be outside forces fighting the equilibrium. Good leaders realize this, and work diligently to maintain proper attitude, starting with their own.

Take a look around you.
Is your team working well together?
Are they progressing in the right direction?
Are they stable and committed?
Are they excelling?

If not, an adjustment may be needed in order to create the proper attitude. The attitude adjustment needs to start with you as the leader because, as the affirmation indicates, the attitudes of those who follow you are very much a reflection of your own.

"Leaders are responsible for their behavior – it's not dependent on the weather, economy, or time of day."

- Unknown

Let's pilot our leadership planes with excellence – no one wants a pilot with a bad attitude!

A PLAYER WITH A GOOD ATTITUDE

ESPN ran an intensely inspiring story that perfectly illustrates this affirmation. It is the story of O.J. Brigance.

Many of you will remember him as having played for the Baltimore Ravens in the 2001 Super Bowl. He was a force to be reckoned with.

And then, in 2007, tragedy struck. He was diagnosed with Amyotrophic Lateral Sclerosis (A.L.S.), also known as Lou Gehrig's disease. Progressively, the disease has stolen his ability to use his arms, then his ability to walk, and eventually, his ability to talk. But it has not stolen his attitude.

If anyone in the world has an excuse for having a bad attitude, it is certainly O.J. Brigance. And yet, when asked how he was doing, he replied, "I'm doing more than making it. I'm living it to the best of my ability."

Instead of giving up and giving in to a defeatist attitude, O.J. gets up three hours early each day and goes to work as the Senior Advisor to Player Development for the Baltimore Ravens. He is a key player on the team, advising players on playing football and even more, on living life to its fullest. And you can bet they listen.

"Regardless of what we go through in life,
there is always purpose wrapped within the pain."

– O.J. Brigance

A PROPRIETOR WITH A GOOD ATTITUDE

A leader's attitude can make or break an organization. A story recently conveyed to me illustrates this point so well, I wanted to share. There are two sandwich shops in this particular area.

A couple went into the first shop, and they had to stand at the counter for several minutes as the two ladies behind the counter hovered around the checkout area complaining amongst themselves. The atmosphere was thick with negativity, so much so that the couple almost walked out without ordering. Finally, one clerk came over to take the order, put a fake smile on her face, and muttered, "What do you want?"

Then, she announced loudly to other clerk that she was trying to have a good attitude. With a sigh, she began to fill the order. There was absolutely no passion in the service. As the couple got to the checkout area, they encountered the other lady. This lady had an even worse attitude – she took the money, shoved the order to the couple, and without a word, walked away.

Contrast that to an experience this couple had at a different restaurant a few days earlier. They walked in and were immediately greeted by smiling faces and a "How may we help you?" They placed their order and made their way down the line, all along the way meeting with smiling faces and eager service providers. They sat down to await the order, and it was brought to their table. As they ate, a man came over and greeted them personally, welcomed them to the shop, and handed them a coupon for their next visit. He asked how the service was in such a way that indicated he really wanted to know and wasn't just collecting surveys. They visited for a bit, and then were surprised to learn that he was the owner of the business. He told them how he hired specific employees because of their people skills and how important it was for him to create a welcoming atmosphere in his restaurant.

Which of these two businesses will that couple visit the next time? And which will they recommend to friends?

A leader with a great attitude who chooses employees with great attitudes directly affects the company's bottom line. Healthy attitudes create healthy businesses. If you want to see unprecedented success in your organization, cultivate an attitude of excellence and service. People *will* notice.

"I am still determined to be cheerful and happy, in whatever situation I may be; for I have also learned from experience that the greater part of our happiness or misery depends upon our dispositions, and not upon our circumstances."

- Martha Washington

POWER REFLECTIONS: This page is provided for the leader in you to reflect on each affirmation and determine how you will apply it to your life and leadership.

_____
_____
_____
_____
_____
_____
_____
_____
_____
_____
_____
_____
_____
_____
_____
_____
_____
_____
_____
_____
_____
_____
_____
_____
_____
_____
_____
_____
_____
_____
_____
_____

Affirmation #2 - Value

Every person alive has value; therefore, I have
a plan to add value to others so as to
accomplish my dreams as a leader.

*"Politeness and consideration for others is like
investing pennies and getting dollars back."*

- Thomas Sowell

AN INVESTMENT WITH REAL VALUE

It has been said that there are only two things on earth that are eternal: the Bible and people. So the question we should all be asking ourselves is, "What are we investing in that truly makes a lasting difference?"

Most of us have invested in the stock market, only to watch our 401k's dwindle to more like 201k's in recent years. Many have invested in homes, only to watch helplessly as the values plummet. Businessmen invest their lives in companies which may or may not exist tomorrow. Doctors and lawyers invest thousands of dollars in an education that may no longer pay off as it once did.

It can all be very discouraging unless our work, however it is defined for each of us as individuals, is based upon the foundation of adding value to people. Money comes and goes, businesses come and go, but the impact a leader has on the lives of his or her people is of lasting value.

I recently heard the story of a lady who served for 33 years as CFO of a large company. She poured her heart and soul into the success of the company, helping to build it from its early beginnings. Though small in stature, she was a force to be reckoned with. And yet, she had an incredible heart for people. It was not uncommon for her to walk out of her office and onto the production floor to talk with the people there about ideas, ask for their advice in areas of their expertise, and visit with them about their interests outside of work as well. It is no wonder that when she retired, the company was thriving and had no debt.

She poured her heart and soul into her family as well, raising four boys and a granddaughter, and spending years researching and writing a family history that reads like a novel. She was successful in business and in art.

Sadly, she was diagnosed with cancer and passed away soon after retiring. Her funeral was attended by board members and factory workers, bankers and bus drivers, family and friends, youngsters and the elderly, and all were there – not just because she was an incredibly successful business woman – but because she had added value to their lives.

As they told their stories, it became clear that the bottom line for her never was just about the numbers – it was about the people with whom she worked and lived.

When it comes down to it, that's about as good as it gets. Do you value those you lead? If you asked the CFO what her best investments were, she would undoubtedly say they were those investments she made in people.

AN INFANTRYMAN WITH REAL VALUE

Nowhere are values more real than on the battlefield. It is there that all the "stuff" of life pales in comparison to the urgency at hand – protecting the lives of those with whom you serve, and fighting for the freedom of those you left behind.

The significance of this affirmation is underscored in the story of Staff Sergeant Clinton L. Romesha. Romesha's awards and decorations are numerous, including the Bronze Star Medal, Purple Heart, and Army Commendation Medal.

But to him, none of that mattered as much as knowing that his fellow infantrymen would be honored for their sacrifice. He understood the value of his comrades in the trenches. And he sought their honor above his own.

Where are you on the battlefield of your business? Are you protecting and honoring your comrades in the trenches, or are you the kind of leader who throws them under the bus? Do you value their lives? Are you fighting for free enterprise and leading your team with the singular focus of serving others?

You must have a build and battle plan. Are you battling along with your team, or are you battling against your team? One thing is certain – if your team is fighting within and not battling the enemy without, victory is well-nigh unattainable.

On the other hand, show me a small force of people, fiercely united for a cause, and fighting together, and victory is almost certain.

"Never doubt that a small group of thoughtful, committed citizens can change the world. Indeed, it's the only thing that ever has."

- Margaret Meade

Victory comes in building the right team, valuing each individual on the team, and fighting with your team against the opposing forces.

AN INDIVIDUAL WITH REAL VALUE

As we have seen, investing in people and creating a committed team is important.

This chapter illustrates the incredible impact that can be made by influencing just one individual.

In the late 1800's, there was a famous evangelist named Dwight L. Moody (D.L. Moody). He is often attributed with a very famous quotation: "The world has yet to see what God can do with one man fully consecrated to him."

The fact is, this was not his quote, but one he referenced often. It inspired him and was a driving force in his life.

The quote was originated by Henry Varley, a British evangelist. Spoken in a conversation with Moody, he thought little of it, but it impacted D.L. Moody deeply – and consequently thousands of others – in ways Mr. Varley could never have imagined.

Driven by this one statement, D.L. Moody was used to influence countless thousands of lives through his sermons, his church, the Moody Bible Institute, Moody Publishers, and his involvement with the Pacific Garden Mission (including the radio broadcast "Unshackled" which airs to this day 12,000 times each week on over 2600 radio outlets.)

In today's environment of mass production, large corporations, broad outreach, and mega-organizations, we should never forget the power of being used to influence one person.

D.L. Moody did indeed reach the masses, but he may not have done so without the influence of that one statement by Henry Varley.

Maybe you are not a D.L. Moody influencing thousands, but perhaps you are a Henry Varley reaching the one who will.

POWER REFLECTIONS: This page is provided for the leader in you to reflect on each affirmation and determine how you will apply it to your life and leadership.

_____
_____
_____
_____
_____
_____
_____
_____
_____
_____
_____
_____
_____
_____
_____
_____
_____
_____
_____
_____
_____
_____
_____
_____
_____
_____
_____
_____

Affirmation #3 - Mission

I am clear about my mission. I spend my time working on and accomplishing what is most important for me.

"A leader's highest power is not the power to hire, fire, or sign checks. A leader's highest power is to create a clear vision of the future that is so compelling that others will enthusiastically help you achieve it."

- Unknown

A LEADER WITH A MISSION

The year was 1962. The place: Rice University, Houston, Texas. It was there on that day the leader of the United States of America, President John F. Kennedy, issued a mission statement – most called it impossible.

Here is that mission:

...But why, some say, the moon? Why choose this as our goal? And they may well ask, why climb the highest mountain? Why, 35 years ago, fly the Atlantic?

We choose to go to the moon. We choose to go to the moon in this decade and do the other things, not because they are easy, but because they are hard, because that goal will serve to organize and measure the best of our energies and skills, because that challenge is one that we are willing to accept, one we are unwilling to postpone, and one which we intend to win....

- President John F. Kennedy, September 12, 1962, at Rice University, Houston, Texas

The mission was set forth, and unprecedented efforts took man to a place that seemed impossible to reach just a decade before. On July 20, 1969, the American astronauts landed on the moon.

Let's look closely at that speech – the speech that sparked one of the most amazing events in world history - to see why it was so effective.

Following are its lessons.

1. If you're going to set goals, set them high. Set them so high that others would label them impossible.

2. Simply define the destination. John C. Maxwell would call this the Law of Navigation.

"A leader is one who sees more than others see, who sees farther than others see, and who sees before others do."

– Leroy Elms

3. Choose. This is a small word, yet huge. Choose…to go. Actively decide to move in the direction of the goal.

4. Set a timeline. This was clearly defined in the mission. The goal would be accomplished within the decade. This is a multi-faceted lesson for leaders. It shows rational thought, long-range planning, and a challenging but reasonable timeline.

5. Organize efforts. Engage the strengths of individuals to create a strong, united team. When the impossible is at stake, "Failure is not an option."

6. Do the hard things. Give it your absolute best effort. Pour your energy into it.

7. Be willing to accept the challenge.

8. Be unwilling to postpone the mission.

9. Intend to win. This is the Law of Intentionality as taught by John C. Maxwell. Wishing to win is not enough Hoping to win is not enough. No, you must INTEND to win. Winning is intentional - on purpose - planned.

The next time you look up at the moon, think of the brave leaders who dared to do the impossible.

And…CHOOSE to aim high.

A LASER-FOCUSED MISSION

Here is a very simple question: How do you spend your time?
Chances are, you spend a great deal of time working.
So the next question would be: What are you working on?

If you listen closely to conversations in this day and age, you will very often hear the word "busy". We are, indeed, a busy society. We move fast, change fast, process information fast, even drive fast and eat fast food, because we are…busy. But are we busy doing the right things, the things that really matter - the things that lead us to accomplish our mission?

Laser focus is absolutely key. A laser is defined in the dictionary as "a device that produces a nearly parallel, nearly monochromatic, and coherent beam of light by exciting atoms to a higher energy level and causing them to radiate their energy in phase." One would think that a small beam of light could not cut through steel, but it does if it is focused.

In our last chapter, we talked about a huge mission. The fact is that mission would have never been accomplished if the massive team had not worked with laser focus. By keeping their mission firmly in front of them at all times, they were able to cut through massive challenges and reach an amazing goal.

Here is how you can have LASER focus.

Let go – You must measure your actions against your mission. In fact, with a clear mission statement, you will know what to say "yes" to, and perhaps more importantly, what to say "no" to.

Anticipate obstacles – No great mission is accomplished without obstacles. Anticipate them, prepare for them, and push through them. The engineers at NASA had manuals full of anticipated problems and solutions, ready at a moment's notice to troubleshoot issues. Those manuals made the difference between disaster and success.

Stay on course – There are a myriad of deterrents at hand these days – television, social media, other people, and more activities than one can imagine. This is why it is essential to stay on course and not allow ourselves to get sidetracked. Do what it takes to focus on the task at hand. Clear your desk of all but the current project, set a timer, turn off email notifications, or simply close the door for a time.

Encourage yourself and your team — There are times in every mission where discouragement rears its ugly head. You, as a leader, must learn to encourage yourself so that you can be an encouragement to your team. Be sure to incorporate times where you recharge your batteries along the way — perhaps take a drive, read a book, have a conversation, rest, do something creative, or take a walk in nature. Never make a critical decision when you are at a point of depletion. Recharge first, and then move forward.

Run! - Have you ever noticed that players who score touchdowns had to run — and fight — to get there? They would never get there if, when handed the ball, they just took off walking. When your mission is defined, run for it. Go for it like you mean it. Score the winning touchdown.

Are you LASER-focused on YOUR mission?

POWER REFLECTIONS: This page is provided for the leader in you to reflect on each affirmation and determine how you will apply it to your life and leadership.

_____
_____
_____
_____
_____
_____
_____
_____
_____
_____
_____
_____
_____
_____
_____
_____
_____
_____
_____
_____
_____
_____
_____
_____
_____

Affirmation #4 - Purpose

Rather than focusing on being successful, I focus on being useful. The latter produces the former.

"So, let us not be blind to our differences - but let us also direct attention to our common interests and to the means by which those differences can be resolved."

- John F. Kennedy, 35th President of the U.S.

A NERD MEETS A NEED

Just about everyone wants to be successful. There are myriads of books on the subject. There are success formulas and success conferences and success coaches. Many have found success in just talking about…success.

But you don't find folks flocking to a conference on being "useful" and there is no book called *Ten Steps to a Useful Life*.

Why is this?

It is perhaps because we do not fully understand the meaning of the word "useful". The dictionary describes it as "being of service, serving a purpose, and doing work that supplies common needs."

If you ask ten people what success means to them, you may get ten different definitions, most of which would be related to having unlimited wealth, recognition, or the freedom to do what they want to do with their time. But if you were to ask someone who already has those things how they define success, chances are they would say, perhaps wistfully, that it would be to have a life of useful purpose.

This is why in history there are two kinds of successful people. There are the miserably successful whose lives often come to a sad or tragic end, and there are the truly successful who have amassed fortunes and then spend their days finding ways to give it away.

This is the difference between a Marilyn Monroe and a Bill Gates. Bill Gates did not start out to become one of the richest men in history. He was focused on creating technology that would serve the needs of people around the world. And what did he do when he had amassed a fortune, almost as a byproduct of that? He found a way to use that fortune to serve the needs of people around the world in a different way. He is successful, not because he focused on being successful, but because he focused on being useful.

If you are seeking success, look around for an opportunity to be of service. Focus on that, and you will find true success.

A SALT HEALS A WOUND

You have undoubtedly heard of the Dead Sea. But did you ever stop to wonder why the Dead Sea is...dead?

The Dead Sea is the lowest elevation on land. Waters flow into it, but (here is the key), there is no outlet. Because of this, it is a pool of saline so concentrated that no animal life can exist within it. Most would call it useless.

And yet, King David found refuge there; and in ancient times, it became a health mecca. People to this day visit the Dead Sea from all over the world just to experience what it is like to float on it. And its salts have been used for products ranging from cosmetics to fertilizer.

In life, there are cycles. If you charted the course of your life, you would see high points and low points. Everyone has them. The low points can feel like the lowest places on earth. They may make you feel purposeless...worthless...useless. All the negative rain has fallen on you, it seems, and there is no outlet. Like the Dead Sea, life becomes saturated with SALT (Sadness Anger Loss Tiredness).

It can be disparaging, but we must remember that SALT can serve two purposes – it can destroy the life within or it can preserve and nurture lives without.

How can YOU become the SALT that gives life?

Serve

Even if you don't feel like it (and you won't), find ways to serve the needs of others, maybe not in the way you imagined, but in a new way.

Acknowledge the Situation

Face it squarely. Fix it if you can. Do all you can to climb back to the top side. But if there is nothing you can do to change the situation, you can still change how you feel about it. Either course of action will inspire and breathe life into others.

Let People Come to You for Health and Healing

It is a well-known fact that the greatest help comes from someone who has "been there". Know that the concentration of SALT in your life is exactly what someone may need someday to "float" through a troubled time and find healing.

Take Time to Just Be

In those low points, there will be a time when you have nothing left to give. Give yourself permission to just stop and "be"…be at rest, be alone with the Creator, be with those you hold dear. Very often, it is during those times of just "being" that purpose becomes crystal clear.

Whether in life or in leadership roles, there will be SALT. The important question is: How will you use it? Will you allow the SALT to take or give life, to hurt or heal, to stagnate or support? Will you allow it to destroy the life within or it preserve and nurture lives without?

A PERSON FINDS A PURPOSE

Most people are well acquainted with the classic Frank Sinatra song, "My Way". We tend to think of it as a declaration of independence, a statement of rebellion, or an expression of regret.

But those are simply parts to a greater whole – and that whole is about a person who has lived life for all it was worth – someone who planned and dreamed, charted a course, reached goals, laughed and cried and loved. And most importantly, they lived this life in their own genuine way. And here's the key. We all hear the line "Regrets, I have a few", but we neglect to hear the rest of that refrain, "But then again, too few to mention."

Why so few regrets?

It is answered in the remainder of that verse, "I did what I had to do, and saw it through without exemption."

A successful, purposeful life of little regret is about knowing who you are and living a genuine life – of squeezing each day for all it's worth, of facing the challenges and overcoming the obstacles, of making a meaningful contribution to the lives of others at every opportunity.

Bill O'Reilly tells about a conversation he had with his father as he was dying of cancer. His father expressed regret at not having lived up to his potential. After he lost his father, Bill began to ask others what one regret they had, and the answers fell into two categories: not reaching one's potential and not doing something to help others when they had the chance.

There is wisdom here beyond measure. How would life be different if each of us focused on these two things, beginning today?

Life is a precious gift. May we live each day to our fullest potential and may we serve others at every opportunity. There is no greater success.

POWER REFLECTIONS: This page is provided for the leader in you to reflect on each affirmation and determine how you will apply it to your life and leadership.

_____
_____
_____
_____
_____
_____
_____
_____
_____
_____
_____
_____
_____
_____
_____
_____
_____
_____
_____
_____
_____
_____
_____
_____
_____
_____
_____
_____

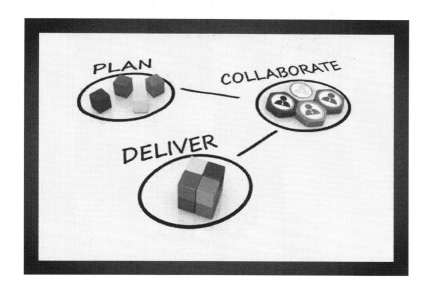

Affirmation #5 - Plan

I have a plan.
I spend time daily developing and
implementing my plan. I do not let busyness
distract me from my plan.

"When you do the things you need to do when you need to do them, the day will come when you can do the things you want to do when you want to do them."

- Zig Ziglar

A LEADER HAS A PLAN

In the Law of Priorities, John C. Maxwell teaches us that leaders understand that activity is not necessarily accomplishment.

We never advance to a point where prioritization is no longer needed. As a matter of fact, I believe it becomes more important the higher we climb up the ladder. We have more people demanding our time and attention, and we have more responsibility - not less - as we grow.

If you are struggling in getting all the important things done on your schedule, I recommend going back to basics. Focus on the Law of Priorities, place the big rocks on your schedule first, and guard this plan with your life.

And remember the advice of one of my favorite mentors:

"When you do the things you need to do when you need to do them, the day will come when you can do the things you want to do when you want to do them."

- Zig Ziglar

A LEADER EXECUTES THE PLAN

Two of the main responsibilities of a leader are very simply these – develop a plan and implement it.

These are elemental to success. If you as a leader are not meeting with success on a regular basis, one of these facets may be missing.

Leaders fall into one of these three categories.

The Ready-Fire-Aim Leader

Ready-Fire-Aim leaders are easy to spot because they are usually running around in crisis mode – crises they themselves have created because they did not create a plan. In the long run, they spend more time repairing than accomplishing.

If this is your tendency, you can break the habit by frequently reminding yourself that creating no plan is creating a crisis. Create the plan and avert the crisis.

The Ready-Ready-Ready-Aim-Aim-Aim...Leader

This is the leader who tries to create the perfect plan only to revise it over and over again because it is not perfect. The perfectionism is rooted in fear. There comes a point where, in order to be an effective leader, one must push through the fear, call it "good enough", and fire. This may not be a natural ability, but it can be learned.

The Ready-Aim-Fire Leader

This is the leader who prepares, plans, and then executes. This is an effective and successful leader. It is the kind of leader who respects the need for a plan but who also knows when to stop planning and take action. This is a balanced leader.

If you find yourself in one of the first two categories, reach out for help. Join an accountability group, engage a mentor, or hire someone who has the skills you need to help you plan or move

forward, as the case may be.
   Learn to be a Ready-Aim-Fire Leader!

A LEADER PLANS AHEAD

One of the most important things we can do as leaders is set the vision for our teams, organizations, and followers. Great leaders are able to internalize mission and vision statements as well as core values and social contract - and then share these with others in such a way they are energized and engaged in the same mission.

Remember, "Leadership is influence - nothing more, and nothing less."

But more than this, it is influencing others toward the key mission of the organization. This may be one of the hardest things to do in leadership, getting others engaged in a mission that ours, but not theirs. So how we do this is the question which must be answered.

In his book *The 21 Irrefutable Laws of Leadership* and the Law of Navigation, John C. Maxwell reminds us to:

P = PREDETERMINE a course of action
L = LAYOUT our goals
A = ADJUST our priorities
N = NOTIFY key personnel

A = ALLOW time for acceptance
H = HEAD into action
E = EXPECT problems
A = ALWAYS point to success
D = DAILY review our plan

"A leader is one who sees more than others see, who sees farther than others see, and who sees before others do."
— Leroy Elms

As leaders, many of us have a knack for seeing what is or what could be in the future. We have knowledge that others don't have due to the position we have within the organization. But position is not enough to lead. We must learn to follow the law of navigation and bring others alongside us to build momentum toward the mission.

POWER REFLECTIONS: This page is provided for the leader in you to reflect on each affirmation and determine how you will apply it to your life and leadership.

_____
_____
_____
_____
_____
_____
_____
_____
_____
_____
_____
_____
_____
_____
_____
_____
_____
_____
_____
_____
_____
_____
_____
_____
_____
_____
_____
_____
_____

Affirmation #6 - Fear

I feel fear and do it anyway,
and I take as many people with me to the top
as possible.

*"You gain strength, courage, and confidence by every
experience in which you really stop to look fear in the face."*

- Eleanor Roosevelt

THERE IS NO WIZARD OF COURAGE

Remember the Cowardly Lion in the Wizard of Oz? He went on a very long journey to find courage. He felt certain the Wizard of Oz would be able to dispense it as a doctor does a prescription and that his fear would suddenly dissipate.

Much to his disappointment, the Wizard was not able to accommodate.

And yet, the Cowardly Lion *did* find courage – not in a gift from the Wizard but from deep within himself. How did he find it? It surfaced when he found a cause greater than his fear – saving his dear friend Dorothy. The cause – the love for his friend – trumped the fear.

Now while this is a fictional story, the principle is solid – *the cause trumps the fear.*

We know what courage looks like.

It is a soldier fighting for the cause of freedom. Courage is firemen and policemen who rushed into those burning towers on September 11, 2001 when others were rushing out. It is a mother who fights all the way to Washington, DC to save the life of her daughter who is two years too young to be on a lung transplant list. It is a Marlene Evans who, while suffering the ravages of cancer and round after round of chemotherapy, continued to teach and counsel ladies with problems which, in reality, paled in significance to hers. It looks like a father who worked harder than any of us can possibly imagine nowadays to support his family during the Great Depression.

These heroes have one thing in common – they are and were courageous. They have another thing in common, too – they experienced fear. What makes them heroes is that they felt the fear but faced it anyway – because they found a cause greater than the fear.

So be encouraged…you have something in common with heroes – you feel the fear.

You have something else in common, too. You have a cause bigger than the fear. Fight for it.

In the Law of Navigation, John C. Maxwell writes that "anyone can steer the ship, but it takes a leader to chart the course." Find your cause, chart the course, face your fears and take others with you to the top.

FEAR AND DO

FEAR and DO - this is a very simple formula for accomplishing something you never dreamed possible.

It is okay to feel the FEAR.
- Fear failure.
- Fear change.
- Fear the unknown.
- Fear controversy.
- Fear obstacles.
- Fear the opinions of others.
- Fear the reactions.
- Fear the humiliation.
- Fear the ridicule.
- Fear the uncertainty.
- Fear the loneliness.
- Fear the cost.
- Fear the responsibilities.

Then DO.

It takes both parts of the equation to succeed. Remember the story of David and Goliath? You can be sure David felt the fear. He was standing in front of a giant with only five stones in his pocket. Others felt the fear, too, but only David had the courage and the faith to push through the fear. He stepped forward and fulfilled his destiny...and he needed only one stone to do it.

So if you find yourself facing a giant with just five stones in your pocket, it is okay to feel the fear. But stepping through it could be the portal to your destiny. And you may find you have more than it takes to do the seemingly impossible.

If you fear without doing, you will get nowhere. It will paralyze you, and you may miss the greatest opportunity of your life.

If you do without fearing, you will be unprepared and ineffective. Fear makes you real and relatable. Overcoming the fear makes you an inspiration.

Feel the fear, and do it anyway – go inspire others.

4 STEPS TO CONQUER FEAR

A few years back, when my son was 6 or 7, we lived in a wooded area. There had been some ferocious dogs running around - at least they were ferocious to my son and his three buddies.

One day, it snowed, and they were home from school. I stayed home from work, and we were out in the woods playing and having snow ball fights. Soon enough, these "kid-eating dogs" began tracking us through the woods. I found an old tree lying down and had the boys hide behind the tree. The dogs were getting closer - they were tracking us down by our smell. The three young boys were scared. I was lying in front of them - their hearts were beating rapidly, and they were breathing hard.

The dogs were getting closer - the boys were beginning to shake with FEAR. The dogs were within 15 or 20 yards of us.

It was time! I jumped up and screamed at the dogs as loudly as I could and began barking at them. They ran off through the woods screaming with their tails tucked and never looked back.

The dogs were gone...no more FEAR. We were all laughing, and my 6-year-old son said, "Daddy, I wet my pants!"

FEAR

False
Evidence
Appearing
Real

Have you had a moment like this in your life, one in which the FEAR was so real, you felt you might tinkle in your pants? I have had many in my life, like the time I chose to go to Air Assault School in the army and rappel from helicopters 130 feet above the ground. I am wet-your-pants scared of heights.

How did I get through this FEAR?

What about Glossophobia - the fear of public speaking? Statistics tell us that public speaking is the number one fear of most people. Up to 75% of the population have Glossophobia. Yes, I had that, too. Jerry Seinfeld got a big laugh when he joked about a survey that found that the fear of public speaking ranks higher in most peoples' minds than the fear of death.

"In other words," he dead-panned, "at a funeral, the average person would rather be in the casket than giving the eulogy."

"The human brain starts working the moment you are born and never stops until you stand up to speak in public."

Because of FEAR, we sometimes become trapped in weak and negative thinking.

*"Our deepest fear is not that we are inadequate.
Our deepest fear is that we are powerful beyond measure.
It is our light, not our darkness, that most frightens us."*

- Nelson Mandela

How do we defeat fear? Let me share 4 steps with you to overcome fear.

Step in. Make today count. Know your purpose. What do you stand for? What are you called to do? Make it a daily goal to STEP IN to your purpose. When we know what our purpose is, FEAR will begin to subside. Visualize the good results of what you want. Do not let your thinking stay stuck in the FEAR of things that most of the time do not happen.

Before speaking, visualize. Picture yourself in the classroom or in the meeting room, standing up, taking your notes to the lectern, and so on. Visualize a successful outcome. Practice. Practice going through your presentation over and over again.

Step forward. Practice successful thinking. Some thinking tips we have to practice include the following:

Embrace reflective thinking. We forget our success, or we do a poor job of learning from others' success. Use journaling.

Feel the energy of possibility thinking. What are the dreams you have for your life? Write them down. Dreams are just dreams until we write them down. Once written, they become aspirations, commitments…goals. Unleash the potential of focused thinking.

Focused thinking harnesses our energy toward a desired goal. Use reflective thinking, remember your goals, and look at them frequently. Continually put yourself on the top of the gold medal podium in your mind, and never give in to the FEAR.

Question the acceptance of popular thinking. What is popular thinking? It is not thinking at all. It is letting others do our thinking for us.

Step across the line. With everything in life, there is a line. On one side of the line is an average, mediocre, and ho-hum life. On the other side, there is a chance for more success. When FEAR creeps in, we have to choose to look across the line and see the chance to succeed. We have to look at others who have chosen to step across the fear line. Each time we choose to cross the line, we begin to build up our resilience, our strength, and our future ability to overcome FEAR the next time it begins to creep in.

Step toward your destiny. Why would Nick Wallenda walk across the Grand Canyon on nothing but a cable? Why would he take that chance? It was his destiny – what he uniquely was made to do. What is your destiny? I truly believe that we are filled with the fuel of our calling, our destiny. We are then more able to STEP THROUGH FEAR.

Every choice we make compounds. The choice to FEAR (Face Everything and Rise) or FEAR (Forget Everything and Run) creates a ripple effect in your life. Your thoughts and actions determine whether or not you fulfill your destiny.

Once you do these things, you, too, will be laughing at the dogs and all the times you came close to wetting your pants!!

POWER REFLECTIONS: This page is provided for the leader in you to reflect on each affirmation and determine how you will apply it to your life and leadership.

_____
_____
_____
_____
_____
_____
_____
_____
_____
_____
_____
_____
_____
_____
_____
_____
_____
_____
_____
_____
_____
_____
_____
_____
_____
_____
_____

Affirmation #7- Mindset

I shape my own destiny.
What I believe, I become;
and I become what I believe.

*"Man often becomes what he believes himself to be.
If I keep on saying to myself that I cannot do a certain thing,
it is possible that I may end by really becoming incapable of
doing it. On the contrary, if I have the belief that I can do it, I
shall surely acquire the capacity to do it, even if I may not
have it at the beginning."*

- Mahatma Gandhi

THE ASSEMBLY LINE OF LIFE

Vision. Mission. _____. _____. Destiny.

You begin with a vision.

Vision itself will not carry you to your destiny. Vision alone is a pipe dream. But add in a defined mission and, suddenly, the impossible starts to take form.

As you can see above, there are two key words missing. And this is where most people get stuck. Those two key points are Belief and Action.

Lack of belief is what makes the difference between an Olympic athlete and the guy who just sits on the bench. Belief will get you off the bench. Believing in the vision will inspire you. Believing the mission is possible will get you started. Believing you can push forward just one more step...and then another...and another will keep you going. And acting on that belief will carry you across the finish line.

Henry Ford said it well, "Whether or not you think you can, you are right."

He not only said it, he lived it. We think of him as being the inventor of the automobile. This is not exactly true. Automobiles already existed. What he did invent was the assembly line, which made the automobile affordable for the common man. Why did he do this? Because he believed there was a way to do what no one else had done before. The belief pulled him into action. He created a system that we rely upon today in just about every manufacturing operation. Henry Ford's destiny was to create the automobile industry.

That destiny came about because of action based on belief based on a mission based on a vision. In essence, Vision-Mission-Belief-Action-Destiny is the assembly line of life, and every stage matters.

Right in the middle of the line is Belief.

Do you believe in your vision enough to carry it to destiny?

THE CONFIDENCE KEY

One of the biggest obstacles most people face is lack of self-confidence. They have a hard time believing what they could accomplish if they only tried – and so, many never try.

Think about it. What opportunities are you missing because you don't believe enough to try? What would you try if you *knew* you would not fail? If you *knew* your business would succeed, would you start it? If you *knew* you would get that dream job, would you apply for it? If you *knew* you could create a masterpiece, would you pull out your paintbrush?

There are three keys to overcoming lack of self-confidence.

Turn off the voices.

Ask yourself where those limiting beliefs are coming from. Are there abusive voices in your past that still control your life? Stop listening! Are the abusive voices you hear coming from you? Stop speaking to yourself that way!

Take just one small step in the right direction.

If you find yourself not trying because you do not believe you could succeed, break the pattern...just once. Pick up the paintbrush, apply for the job, start the business. Sometimes you have to take action before the belief starts to unfold. Go ahead...take just one step toward that mission you feel compelled to pursue. You might not be able to see it now, but success could very well be right around the next bend. We've all heard the saying, "I'll believe it when I see it." The reality is more that you will see it when you believe it. And believing begins when you take that first step.

"If you start today to do the right thing, you are already a success,
even if it doesn't show yet."

— John C. Maxwell

Try again.

If your hesitation to start is based on fear of failure, let me assure you that you *will* fail. Now that we have that settled, let me also assure you that failure is simply part of the learning process. Success comes to those who learn from failure, adjust course, and take another step. John C. Maxwell says, "The only guarantee for failure is to stop trying." Fear stopping more than failing.

Turn off the voices, take that first step, and get back up when you fall down. These are the tenants of belief…and that is the basis for success.

THE HAPPYNESS KEY

A few years ago, a very compelling movie made its debut. *The Pursuit of Happyness* was based on the real life story of Chris Gardner who went from being homeless to being a millionaire. Chris had all the odds stacked against him from an early age; and the reality is, he had plenty of legitimate excuses for failing – yet he refused to give up. He believed he could succeed. He believed he could learn what he needed to learn to do the job he needed to do to earn the living he wanted to live. He believed he could be the father to his son that his father could not be to him. And he did it.

I saw an interesting quote recently, though I'm not sure who said it: "Give up, give in, or give it all you've got."

Chris Gardner gave it everything he had. And in doing so, he not only changed his own life in phenomenal ways, he changed the course of his family for generations to come.

So let me ask you: how are your beliefs and actions affecting those who follow in your footsteps? We who are parents, especially, carry a heavy responsibility to show our children how to overcome doubts and obstacles. There are few greater life lessons than those.

MICHAEL H. HARBOUR II

There is a famous poem that illustrates this affirmation well.

The Man Who Thinks He Can
By Walter D. Wintle

If you think you are beaten, you are;
If you think you dare not, you don't.
If you'd like to win, but think you can't
It's almost a cinch you won't.

If you think you'll lose, you've lost,
For out in the world we find
Success being with a fellow's will;
It's all in the state of mind.

If you think you're outclassed, you are:
You've got to think high to rise.
You've got to be sure of yourself before
You can ever win a prize.

Life's battles don't always go
To the stronger or faster man,
But soon or late the man who wins
Is the one who thinks he can.

Be one who thinks you can.

"If you believe you can, you probably can. If you believe you won't, you most assuredly won't. Belief is the ignition switch that gets you off the launching pad."

-   Denis Waitley

POWER REFLECTIONS: This page is provided for the leader in you to reflect on each affirmation and determine how you will apply it to your life and leadership.

_____
_____
_____
_____
_____
_____
_____
_____
_____
_____
_____
_____
_____
_____
_____
_____
_____
_____
_____
_____
_____
_____
_____
_____
_____
_____
_____
_____
_____

Affirmation #8 - Example

Leaders raise the bar.
As I go, so goes my team, my department, my organization. I will constantly and consistently grow toward excellence.

"Excellence is a better teacher than mediocrity.
The lessons of the ordinary are everywhere.
Truly profound and original insights are to be found only in studying the exemplary."

- Warren G. Bennis

RAISE THE BAR

Let me ask you a question: Are you a better leader today than you were a year ago?

Probably much like you who are reading this, I have spent most of my years in some sort of leadership role. However, what I have learned as I have had more people responsible to me is that I have to grow as a leader if I want my influence to grow.

John C. Maxwell defines leadership as "influence, nothing more and nothing less".

I believe John is right, but what kind of influence is the important question. I have experienced many types of influence in the jobs I have had over my career and as a leadership coach, speaker, and trainer. I have witnessed both great influencers and negative influencers. The scary part is most of the negative influencers were not aware of their negative leadership. This is sad, really.

Are you aware of your influence? Are you aware of your strengths that make you a good leader, but that may also be limiting your influence if not used correctly?

There are four things every leader must do to grow in their leadership effectiveness. In John C. Maxwell's book *The 21 Irrefutable Laws of Leadership*, John says our leadership effectiveness will only rise to the level of our ability. In other words, we have to raise the lids of our leadership.

Step 1 is getting REAL. Get real about our lids, our strengths, our weaknesses, and our influence.

Step 2 is getting CLEAR about who we want to be as leaders. What is your vision of where you want to take your team, family, and followers? What is the legacy you want to leave?

Step 3 is getting SMART about how we can overcome the limiting factors in our influence. From whom do you need to learn and who do you need to study to grow in your ability?

Step 4 is getting a WIND UP CLOCK. What got us here will not get us where we want to go. We must follow the law of process and make a daily commitment to grow and continue to raise our lids as leaders.

Our world - our communities - our companies - our followers...all of them are screaming for leadership.

Sometimes major change begins with just one person – one influential leader. Will *you* be that one person? And will your influence be the right kind of influence?

Decide today to be a world changer, and begin with your circle of influence.

SET THE COMPASS

I have used a compass as a part of my logo almost since the inception of Harbour Resources (www.harbourresources.com). It has become a symbol for me and everything I do to add value to my clients, potential clients, friends, my family, and community. The compass is always pointed toward true north.

What I didn't say above is that I am always pointed toward true north. As a leader of my business, my family, and a leader in my church and community, I sometimes lose focus and get off track. I lose my way at times.

What about you? Do you ever lose your way?

I work with leaders in many different industries. I talk with leaders all over the world. And I have been mentored by and still am being mentored by great leaders like John Maxwell, Les Brown, and Paul Martinelli, just to name a few. I am in close association with these leaders on a regular basis.

What I have learned from every one of the leaders I connect with is that getting off track is human. You see, we are not like a bunch of cows just following the same old beaten path every single day. No. We are creators, explorers, and doers. We are designed in the image of the Grand Overall Designer who has wired us to make things happen. As leaders, we get bored if we are not doing something. If I don't have anything to do - which is rare - I will tear something up just to have something to do. I get off track sometimes!

So, what does the compass have to do with this anyway? Well, for me, and you, too, I am sure, we have to have a way back to who we are as a leader. We get lost, but the compass helps us find our way back.

If you have ever heard me speak or teach, or have watched any of my videos, you will frequently hear me reference my 4 Corner Posts. They are: Get Real, Get Clear, Get Smart, and Get a Wind-Up Clock.

The compass contains two of these corner posts. First, we have to stop and Get Real about being off track - being lost and off course from our goals and vision for ourselves and our teams. And secondly, we have to Get Clear about the direction we want to go next.

As leaders, if we are headed in the wrong direction and don't get clear about the change we need to make to reset our compass, we will keep getting further off track.

And we all know the old definition of insanity:

"If we keep on doing what we have always been doing, then we will keep on getting what we have always gotten."

Here is the lesson: as leaders, we will make mistakes. We will get off track. We will get lost. Even the greatest leaders I know have made big mistakes. If we are not making mistakes and being criticized, then we probably aren't leading. However, don't be afraid to fail, make mistakes, and be authentic to who you are as a leader. You were wired to lead. Embrace this strength and keep leading!

When you get off track, stop, and Get Real.

Reset your compass, and Get Clear about the change in direction you need to make.

And don't ever stop leading.

The world is screaming for leadership – and someone needs to answer the call. It might as well be you!

OVERCOME THE OBSTACLES

At a John Maxwell event and speaker training seminar in Orlando, Florida. I listened to some powerful speeches by Les Brown (Motivational Speaker, Speech Coach, and Best-Selling Author), Nick Vujicic (http://www.lifewithoutlimbs.org/), and Paul Martinelli (http://paulmartinelli.net/). I listened intently as each told his respective story and as they taught us, based on their combined decades of experience. I guess you could say, I was "studying the exemplary" as Warren G Bennis quotes at the beginning of this chapter.

I studied their methods, their words, their presentation skills…but what stood out more than anything else were the men and their messages. The message of Les Brown: "It's possible." The message of Paul Martinelli: "You have the potential." And the resounding message of Nick Vujicic: "You can overcome the pain."

Each of these men faced obstacles. In Nick's case, the obstacles are unfathomable. But he did not give up. Nick tells how his parents had to firmly extend "tough love" in order for him to learn to do what he does today. When he cried for something, his mom would say, "Get it yourself." I have to think there were many times she had to turn her head to hide the tears as she said that. But she knew that with Nick's level of disability, he would have to learn ways to do things others would deem impossible. So, little by little, Nick's parents raised the bar. They held him to a high standard. They pushed. And most of all, they loved. He will tell you that the reason he can do what he does today – and in fact the reason he is even alive today - is because of his parents. They led him to excellence.

If anyone in the world has a deck of excuse cards for doing nothing in life, it is Nick Vujicic. But he refuses to play the game.

In one exercise, Nick has the audience list their three main limitations (a.k.a. "excuses"). This is challenging to do when you're looking at someone with no arms and no legs who is living a full and purposeful life. All of a sudden, it starts to give you some real perspective. He goes on to ask a compelling question: "What would happen in your life if there were some way, somehow, some means to overcome each of those limitations?" And as select members of the audience chose to share their three limitations, it starts to become apparent. It is not the circumstance that creates the limitation; it is the person creating his or her own limitation.

Circulating back to the messages of Paul Martinelli and Les Brown…the possibilities are out there, and you have the potential to do more than you ever imagined.

And if you don't believe that, look up Nick Vujicic's website.

So…now…what was that excuse you had?

"The things you want are always possible; it is just that the way to get them is not always apparent. The only real obstacle in your path to a fulfilling life is you, and that can be a considerable obstacle because you carry the baggage of insecurities and past experience."

- Les Brown

POWER REFLECTIONS: This page is provided for the leader in you to reflect on each affirmation and determine how you will apply it to your life and leadership.

_____
_____
_____
_____
_____
_____
_____
_____
_____
_____
_____
_____
_____
_____
_____
_____
_____
_____
_____
_____
_____
_____
_____
_____
_____
_____
_____
_____
_____
_____
_____
_____

Affirmation #9 - Strengths

A leader's primary role is to equip people to use their gifts. I will place people in their strengths zone and step out of their way so we are all successful.

"If your actions create a legacy that inspires others to dream more, learn more, do more, and become more, then you are an excellent leader."

- Dolly Parton

TRAINING TREES AND BUILDING A LEGACY

One of our annual traditions is to take a picture of our children on their first day of school.

The last time we took that picture, it hit me – they are growing up way too fast.

Sooner than I care to think about, those pictures will be of high school and college graduations – weddings and grandchildren. As a father, part of me wants them always to be young and under my care, but I know they are only young for a season.

That picture was a reminder of the responsibility I carry for training my children "in the way they should go". To me, that means helping them explore and discover their gifts and then equipping them with the tools they need to use those gifts to serve the world. It means instilling in them solid principles for life.

If you've ever planted a tree, you know that very often, you have to put stakes in the ground and tie ropes to the tree from several directions to give it support. You are "training" the tree to stand tall and straight. You are anchoring it because it is just too small to stand up to the elements. You carefully nurture and protect it. After a time, you see that the tree is growing and strong...and you know it is time to pull up the stakes and cut the rope. Keeping them attached will only constrict growth. The storms will come, but if you have done your job well, the tree will stand strong and continue to grow and prosper. It will grow taller than you, and someday you will stand under the shade of its canopy...and remember how small and fragile it once was.

Just as we train trees in the way they "should go", we are responsible to train those precious souls under our care. And notice that verse doesn't say train them in the way we "want" them to go, because each person is unique. Often, I encounter people in careers that just do not fit them simply because a parent told them they should pursue that career. So not only did they not get the support they needed to grow into their strengths...they grew up being told they were the wrong kind of tree!

I see leaders as those who train the trees. And I see legacy as the day a leader can stand in a forest and find that the trees he once planted are providing a canopy of protection for seedlings of their own. And then he realizes that those little trees he once protected and nurtured are now protecting him.

And so for now, I go to ball games and root for my son, and I dance with my daughter at the daddy-daughter dances. I spend my nights helping with homework and my days working to support my family. I smile and weep and pray...and I realize - with great gravity - that I am building a legacy.

The Law of Legacy reminds us that a leader's lasting value is measured by succession. Are you going to leave a legacy?

5 STEPS EVERY LEADER SHOULD TAKE

Many people see the role of a leader as being the one who knows it all and does it all. The reality is quite the opposite. Great leaders are smart enough to know they don't know it all. In fact, the best leaders are those who surround themselves with a trusted team of people who have strengths where they are weak. The job of a leader is not to have all the answers or do all the work. The job of a leader is to assemble and equip a team that, collectively, can do more than the leader could possibly do as an individual.

The best step a leader can take is very often stepping away...so the most qualified person on the team can step up to the plate.

Here are five steps every leader should take:

Step away from day-to-day tasks.

If you as a leader are doing all the work, three things will happen: (1) There will be no leadership; (2) The work will not get done (you are, after all, just one person); and (3) Your team will be weak and co-dependent.

Step into the broader perspective.

Your job is not to micromanage. Your job is to assemble, train, and equip a team that does not require micromanagement. If you find yourself micromanaging, you have failed as a leader in one these key areas. Your job is to constantly see the organization from the broader perspective and to ensure the team is working together toward the goals that have been set.

Step out of your comfort zone.

If you have started a company, it feels like your baby. You have labored and given birth to it, and now it has grown to a point where you have to start letting go a bit in order for it to grow further. If you are like most entrepreneurs, you started out doing everything yourself...and now you have to entrust your baby to the care of others. This is not comfortable. But it is necessary. If

60

you've done your job well, there will be frequent intervals where you have to let go of something you are doing in order to reach the next level. Prepare to step out of your comfort zone on a regular basis.

Step up to a higher level.

As a leader, you must continually push to higher levels. Push yourself and your team to do more and be more. Be a continual learner. Ask questions, look for new opportunities, and take advantage of training opportunities. And encourage your team to do the same. As you move to a higher level, it allows your team to progress as well.

Step aside.

The fifth step is to step aside and let your team shine. Recognize their individual strengths and look for opportunities that will allow them to work in those areas of strength. Be sure to give credit where credit is due. I see a good leader as one who gains the spotlight and then turns it to the team member or members who made it possible. Step aside, leaders...and let those who did the work take the bow.

POSITIONING YOUR PLAYERS

A good leader will recognize each team member's individual gifts and will encourage the use of those gifts.

We all have seen scenarios where someone is good at a particular skill – let's say, internet technology, for example. Recognizing those skills and wanting to reward them, a manager may promote this gifted technology person to the level of Internet Technology Director. On the surface, this is a logical progression, and the employee should be thrilled with the promotion. Only...that is not always the case. In some instances, the employee will go into a silent panic mode. Being dedicated, he or she will try to make it work; but the fact is, they may not be as comfortable dealing with people and budgets as they are in dealing with computers.

And so they begin to fail.

The sad part is that often the employee ends up being let go when the fault ultimately lies with the leader who failed to equip the employee with the tools needed to do the job. Just because a person is good at IT doesn't mean they are good with people. There are skills that can be taught, and there are some for whom such a promotion will never work. And it is the leader's responsibility to know the difference.

How do you ensure your team players are suited up and playing in the correct positions for them?

Know your players.

I'm reminded of the quote from the movie *The Blind Side* where Leigh Anne Touhy told Coach Cotton: "You should really get to know your players, Coach. Michael scored in the 98th percentile in protective instincts." Because she knew Michael, she was able to coach him in a way that he understood. Knowing your players opens avenues for teaching and communication in ways they can understand and apply. You have to know your players.

Equip your players.

There are a lot of discussions these days on helmet safety in an effort to determine if more can be done to alleviate concussions and their long-term health effects. Can you imagine how bad the injuries would be if we still used the old leather helmets?

We as leaders are responsible for safely equipping our players before sending them off to a game. If you are setting someone up as a manager or director, have you provided them the training they need to do the job?

Place your players in the proper positions.

No pro football coach I know would even think to place a quarterback in the linebacker position or vice versa. Those two positions require totally different skills and body mass. A good coach knows if you place them in the wrong positions, two things will happen – someone will get hurt, and the team will lose.

There is tangible value in knowing your players, equipping your players, and placing them in the proper positions. This is how you can create an "A" team.

POWER REFLECTIONS: This page is provided for the leader in you to reflect on each affirmation and determine how you will apply it to your life and leadership.

_____
_____
_____
_____
_____
_____
_____
_____
_____
_____
_____
_____
_____
_____
_____
_____
_____
_____
_____
_____
_____
_____
_____
_____
_____
_____
_____

Affirmation #10 - Influence

The power, influence, and confidence I seek
come from my security in who I am, in my
identity as a leader. I will not my let
insecurities create weakness in my influence.

*"Regardless of how you feel inside, always try to look like a
winner. Even if you are behind, a sustained look of control
and confidence can give you a mental edge that results in
victory."*

- Diane Arbus

DETERMINE THE OBSTACLES

In a conference, Nick Vujicic conducted an interesting exercise. He had everyone in the audience write down the three biggest things they wanted to accomplish in life, with emphasis on big things, not just small goals. These are the kinds of things that almost seem impossible. Then he had everyone write down the three reasons they couldn't possibly do those things. I call those excuses.

I challenge you to do this before you read further.

As a few from the audience read their "excuses", it became apparent. We are capable of much more than we realize, and our excuses are more often than not related to one major obstacle: ourselves!

One obstacle that surfaced several times was lack of confidence - insecurity based on fear. This holds more people back than anything. What if I do this, and it doesn't work? What if I try this, and I fail? What if people laugh at me? What if I try to win…and I lose? All of these are fears based on a lack of confidence.

The fact is, we all have fears. Even the strongest leaders deal with insecurities. In fact, those in the audience – those expressing fear and insecurity - were known for being strong and influential leaders.

Leaders who accomplish big dreams and goals are those who feel the fear and insecurity, take a deep breath, and face them head on.

Keep in mind as you feel the insecurities, hear the voices of doubt in your mind, and sense the fear of failure – that more often than not, your biggest dreams lie just on the other side. Push through.

You have what it takes to do more than you think.

DITCH THE APPROVAL RATINGS

This affirmation comes at a time when our country is facing major issues on all fronts, our nation's economy verges on default, and our leaders can't seem to…well…lead.

There comes a time when a leader has to make the right decisions – not based on popularity or politics or whether or not someone's feelings will get hurt. The fact is, you can't please all the people all the time. As a leader, you have to be able to negotiate and work with people who may have different views than you, people who have different personalities – and solve problems.

It has been said that the best approach is to attack the issues and not each other. This advice works well in homes, churches, and it should also work in the government of our country. In a time like this, our leaders need to be working together to resolve the issues our country faces, not worrying about approval ratings.

As leaders in our individual realms of home, work, ministry, and community, it would serve us well to ditch approval ratings and just resolve to do what is wise and what is right in any given situation.

If you and your spouse have an issue, do what's right. If you disagree with someone in your church or workplace, do what's right. If you serve in the government, do what's right.

Insecure leaders are weak leaders. We will all feel the insecurity at times, but we must not allow it to become the defining factor of our influence.

Whoever you are, wherever you serve…ditch approval ratings and simply do what's right.

DEAL WITH THE INSECURITY

There is a common characteristic of many highly successful business leaders and pro-athletes that may surprise you. When you see them speaking to large audiences, being interviewed by the media, or playing in the Super Bowl, you may think they have all the confidence in the world. They appear strong, poised, and driven, when quite the opposite may be true. Many of them share the common characteristic of insecurity.

The fact is, the more you are geared toward excellence, the more you will feel the insecurity. But the secret to success is learning to use that insecurity to the advantage of you and your team. Three-time Super Bowl winner Tom Brady attributes insecurity to his success. He once said, "I guess I always feel there's someone hunting me down, someone right on my footsteps."

If you feel that way, you are in good company.

How do you use insecurity as a help instead of a hindrance?

Acknowledge that you will have those feelings.

Somehow just knowing the feelings are normal gives you a sense of acceptance. Insecure leaders who do not understand this come across as overbearing micro-managers. They tend to put undue pressure on their team to make themselves look good to their superiors.

Play through.

Feel the insecurity, but do the job anyway. Caving in not only makes you feel even more insecure; it also causes your team to lose confidence in your leadership. So, really, you have no choice but to play through.

Feeling the insecurity but working through it makes you a relatable leader. Those who follow you will be inspired to work through their insecurities as well.

Use it to propel you forward.

If you feel as Tom Brady that someone is always nipping at your heels, it will keep you moving forward. If you're running from someone or something, be sure you are headed in the right direction – because if you run long enough from the insecurity, you will end up reaching your goal.

You hear a lot about the high cost of insecurity. But as you can see here, there is high value in insecurity if you use it as a tool for your success.

POWER REFLECTIONS: This page is provided for the leader in you to reflect on each affirmation and determine how you will apply it to your life and leadership.

Affirmation #11 - Growth

What got me here will not take me where I want to go in the future. I am continually sharpening my saw, learning from others, and surrounding myself with people who stretch me to a new level.

"If one advances confidently in the direction of his dreams, and endeavors to live the life which he has imagined, he will meet with success unexpected in common hours."

- Henry David Thoreau

71

DREAM BIG

I have a friend who dreams big. She grew up in a broken home. There were tough times – really tough – but even then, she dreamed big. She dreamed of someday having a yellow house with a white porch and a single dormer at the top.

As she became an adult, she refined the dream, adding on an extension to the side and making a very detailed, visionary list – a home with small acreage near a town but in the country, a sunken living room, a bay window, and a wall of windows…an older house but with newer wiring and plumbing and a solid foundation.

It seemed to be an impossible dream. But she kept the vision in front of her – literally a picture from a magazine on the refrigerator. And she and her husband prayed and worked hard.

Those three elements came together one fateful day as they spotted a beautiful house that looked just like the picture on the refrigerator, and it "just happened" to be for sale. The story of how they came across that house and how they were able to get it is amazing. As they stepped off the porch after first viewing it, her husband said, "It would be a miracle if we got this house." And so it was nicknamed "the miracle house" because they did, indeed, get it.

This story illustrates the power of vision – the power of believing in it, praying for it, working toward it…and never giving up, even though it appears to be impossible.

I challenge you this week to DREAM BIG. Dream in detail until you have a very clear vision. Ignore the voices of doubt and discouragement, and just put it out there – right on your refrigerator where you can't miss it. And then do your part – pray, believe, and work toward that vision. You may be quite surprised at the outcome.

Dreaming is not enough. You must take action. Where is the picture of YOUR vision posted, and what are you doing to make it happen?

4 CORNER POSTS TO GROWTH

Let me ask you a few questions.

Would you pay full price for a 50-year-old house that has not been cleaned, maintained, or updated since it was built? Would you go to a doctor who graduated from medical school 50 years ago but has not studied or practiced medicine or taken any classes since completing his or her original studies? Would you go to a dentist who still uses the dental tools and methods of that era? Would you use 50-year-old technology to run your critical business operations today?

Of course not!

As important as it is to keep a house, certifications, tools, and technology up to date in order to maintain value, it is even more important that we keep working on ourselves in order to maintain our value.

The fact is, we have to keep moving forward in life, or we start to fall behind. If we are moving forward and growing, we are better equipped to participate in the opportunities that come our way.

Here are four corner posts to growing ourselves in a way that brings value to those we serve:

Get Real – Take a good hard look at where you are. Is it where you want to be? Look at each area of life and give it a score on a scale of 1-10. How are you…spiritually, physically, emotionally, and financially? How are your relationships? Are your career skills up to date? This exercise is not to make you feel badly about any one part, but it is necessary to get real about what's working and what's not working.

Get Clear – Look at all areas that scored 5 or below, and ask yourself which one area – if you changed it for the better – would be most impactful on your life as a whole. Just choose one for now.

Get Smart – Write that one area down and then create a smart plan of 1-3 steps you can take within the next 90 days to begin to turn it around. Let's say, for instance, you have a $1000 credit card bill. Could you pay it off in 90 days? Absolutely. Break it down. If you can save or generate just $350 a month, you will pay it off before the 90 days passes. If you have packed on 25 extra pounds, and it is starting affect your health, you have time in just 90 days to turn it around. Breaking it down and laying out a specific plan is a smart way to accomplish your goals. Think about it. If you do nothing, your problem will be compounded in 90 days. Conversely, if you simply create a plan and stick to it for 90 days, it could be eradicated. GONE! Totally gone. Now the big question: Which scenario feels better? And why would you choose *not* to do it?

Get a wind-up clock – You know what area you need to improve upon. You have a plan that you know will work if you simply do it day by day for 90 days. Most people get this far. But then something happens – they get tired, circumstances arise, negative thoughts and doubts come, self-sabotage occurs – and they stop. Their momentum clock winds down. If you find yourself at this point, don't be discouraged. It is normal. But you must take action to rewind your clock. Get reinforcements, read inspirational and motivational books, do something physical to get your energy back, rest for a specified time, talk with a mentor or coach...whatever you do, find a way to rewind the clock and get back on course within a day or two. Make sure going into this you have an accountability partner who will not let you quit.

Now let me ask you those questions again. Would you buy a 50-year-old house that had been meticulously maintained and updated through the years...which had grown with its surroundings into a beautifully landscaped classic? Would you choose a doctor who had graduated with honors and who had grown his or her skills and experience through the years to an expert level in his or her field? Would you go to a dentist who had the old-school skills plus the new school technologies in his tool kit? Would you use the technologies developed by NASA combined with new technology to run your business?

That is the difference between growing old...and growing. You get to choose...starting today.

4 IMPORTANT WORKOUTS

I will be the first to admit that I do not like to exercise. I do not wake up every morning like some of my friends with great anticipation for jumping on a treadmill or doing 300 pushups before breakfast. Nevertheless, I do make time for physical activity because I know that my body is the vehicle to carry me where I need to go, and I must maintain it.

Having a vision and fulfilling a dream is like good health — we enjoy it. Getting there...well, it is a lot like exercise. We may not enjoy it, but we must focus on the results, which we certainly will enjoy.

Here are 4 Important Workouts to help us reach our goals and fulfill our dreams.

Pull-Ups — If you've ever started an exercise regimen from couch-potato status, you know that when doing those first pull-ups, your body weight is against you. For one thing, you weigh more because you haven't been working out; and for another, your muscles are slack. But as you do those pull ups each day, they start to get easier. Your arms get stronger, and your weight gets lighter.

When we set out to reach a goal, those first steps will be the most difficult. We can't see how we can possibly get there. It's grueling. We feel the weight of the world on our shoulders. But we push...and before long, we can look back and realize how far we've come. We are lighter and stronger, and the goal that seemed impossible just a few days before is now visible on the horizon.

Push-Ups — Push-ups require a strong core. Pushing toward your goal requires a strong core as well. It requires that you know who you are and what your abilities are. You can't run someone else's race — you have to run yours. Knowing who you are keeps you on track to do what is most important to you.

Intervals — Interval workouts involve pushing yourself to the limit, holding for a time, then resting. To reach your goals, you must work hard — really hard. And then give yourself periods of rest to recharge your battery. Many people take one of two paths —

they either rest all the time or work with full intensity all the time. Ironically, either path will get you to the same place – a heart attack. Push hard, yes, but always take time to get back to center as well. Keep life in balance.

Stretches – Every fitness expert will tell you that stretching is important. This helps keep your muscles from locking up on you. Stretching yourself in other areas of life is important, too. Mental, spiritual, vocational, social, financial, and educational stretching is necessary. Are your relationships strained? You will need to stretch there, too, by reaching out to the other person to keep the relationship strong. If some area of your life is in lockdown…stretch. Reach out to someone who can help you over an obstacle. Reach out to learn what you need to know. Reach out to take just one uncomfortable step forward.

So there you have it…some pretty good fitness advice from someone who hates to exercise. 'Care to join my exercise program?

"And the day came when the risk to remain tight in a bud was more painful than the risk it took to blossom."

— Anaïs Nin

POWER REFLECTIONS: This page is provided for the leader in you to reflect on each affirmation and determine how you will apply it to your life and leadership.

_____
_____
_____
_____
_____
_____
_____
_____
_____
_____
_____
_____
_____
_____
_____
_____
_____
_____
_____
_____
_____
_____
_____
_____
_____
_____
_____
_____
_____
_____

Affirmation #12 - Excellence

Excellence is getting just a little bit better each day, month and year. I will spend time reflecting on the last year and learn from my success - and design the way forward so next year is my best year ever.

"Few people are willing to stop being what they are, to be what they want."

— Dr. Gene Landrum

MICHAEL H. HARBOUR II

WHAT'S ON YOUR QUIT LIST?

We all live very busy lives. It seems one day we're looking at our calendar, and it is January 1 with all its hopes for a grand new year…and the next, it is 11:59 p.m. on December 31, and the year is about to end. And we are left wondering what happened in between to all those things we had planned to do.

And so we do as we did the year before and hastily scribble down a few vague resolutions (which look very much like the previous year's hastily scribbled vague resolutions). These last about two weeks into the new year and then fade back into obscurity.

I urge you to decide now, no matter what day in the year it is, to stop being what you are and start becoming who you were meant to be. I urge you to take a little time to reflect on the year thus far. Write down what worked well…and also what did not. Write down what you are doing that fits you and your purpose…and write down what gnaws at you as you try to sleep at night.

These are indicators of what to keep and what to change. Dan Miller, the highly successful best-selling author of *48 Days to the Work You Love* and *No More Dreaded Mondays* does this every year. He maps out his goals for the year, and he decides not only what he will do…but also what he will stop doing.

Look at each area of life (Physical Health, Spiritual Health, Mental Health, Work, Finances, Relationships, and Home) and for each area, list what worked and what did not.

Of what did not work, ask yourself if it makes sense to fix it. If not, then it needs to go on your QUIT list. Don't fool yourself into thinking you need to keep on doing all that you're doing. The fact is, sometimes you need to stop doing a few of those things in order to move forward.

A good leader knows when to quit.

What's on *your* quit list?

WHAT'S ON YOUR DREAM BOARD?

Each year, my wife and I work on a very important project together. We build our Dream Board. Personally, I think all couples would benefit from doing this once a year.

What if you sat down together and just dreamed – no holds barred – just put it out there. Most people hesitate to do this because they think it will never happen, so why bother.

But I can tell you from experience that three things will happen:

(1) You won't accomplish all that is on your Dream Board, and that's okay;

(2) You will accomplish much more than you would accomplish if you didn't do this; and

(3) You will most likely be surprised that at least one ends up totally surpassing your expectations.

So, go ahead, dream big. Put it out there: pictures, words, symbolic objects. Make it tangible. Think of each area of your life and what your dream is for it – spiritual, physical, relationships, home, career, finances…things you enjoy, places you want to go, people you want to help. Put it on the board, and put the board where you will see it daily. There is something about "seeing" something that tricks your mind into believing the impossible might just be possible. As you pass by the board each day, something will catch your eye, and it will remind you to take just one more little step. If you do that enough, you'll be 365 steps closer to your dream this time next year than you are this year.

I challenge you to do this...do it yourself or with your spouse, family, or company. And then send me an email as you start to see the impossible unfold. Or better yet, take us for a ride in your Maserati when you get it!

WHAT'S ON YOUR PRIORITY LIST?

This is the very last chapter in the 12 Great Affirmations series. It is hard to believe we have come this far already, but the fact that we have done so actually illustrates the value of today's final lesson – the importance of having a PRIORITY LIST.

Prior to the start of this series, I determined it was a priority, and though there were many opportunities for distraction along the way, the fact that this was a priority forced me to make it happen.

It is a good feeling to reach a goal and know that, while you have not been able to accomplish everything, you HAVE been able to accomplish the priorities you set.

Today's fast-paced society being what it is, having a priority list is the ONLY way to be effective. There are endless distractions and demands, and if we don't have the focus of a priority list, we will find ourselves at the end of each year no closer to our goals than when we started. Repeated long enough, we will come to the end of life with nothing to show for it.

In the first segment of this chapter, we talked about the importance of a QUIT list. This is a healthy way to declutter what doesn't fit from our schedules and to-do lists.

In the next segment, we talked about the importance of DREAM board. This is a no-holds barred visual of all the possibilities.

And in this segment, we will talk about the importance of the PRIORITY list. If all you have is a QUIT list, your life will feel empty. If all you have is a DREAM board, your life will feel overwhelming. But if you have a PRIORITY list, you will be able to effectively and efficiently carry out those dreams and maintain a better sense of life balance.

So go back to your DREAM board and ask yourself: Of all those possibilities, what are the three that would be most significant? What three areas of focus would have the most impact? What three would give you a good foothold? But here's the key: THREE.

The reality is, most people can effectively juggle three things at once. They can develop three areas at a time. Beyond that, they tend to lose effectiveness

So look at your DREAM board and choose THREE. Write

these down as your priorities. The key here is to write them down and place them in a prominent place you visit often – on your desk, on the front of your refrigerator, in your car, on the bathroom mirror, or save as your computer wallpaper – or all of the above. Keep them where you can focus on them several times a day.

Then set THREE milestones for each that you can accomplish in the next quarter. You will have three priorities with three milestones in each.

This is a doable plan. If you try to do everything at once, you will fail. But if you target three at a time each quarter, you will be surprised at the end of next year how far you have come.

Each day, take one small step in the direction of each priority. And each evening, evaluate progress.

It has been said that if you don't plan your time, someone else will do it for you. And you may not like their choices. This is your chance to evaluate what is most important to you, and set your priorities.

Come what may, protect those priorities. Believe me, distractions and diversions will arise, but hold your ground. You will encounter obstacles, but focus on priorities. You will be weary, but push toward priorities.

It's your choice. You can try to hit all marks and fail. Or you can focus on priorities and hit a higher level of success than you ever have before.

And if you do nothing, that choice will be made for you.

12 GREAT AFFIRMATIONS FOR LEADERS

AFFIRMATION #1 - ATTITUDE

AFFIRMATION #2 - VALUE

AFFIRMATION #3 - MISSION

AFFIRMATION #4 - PURPOSE

AFFIRMATION #5 - PLAN

AFFIRMATION #6 - FEAR

AFFIRMATION #7 - MINDSET

AFFIRMATION #8 - EXAMPLE

AFFIRMATION #9 - STRENGTHS

AFFIRMATION #10 - INFLUENCE

AFFIRMATION #11 - GROWTH

AFFIRMATION #12 - EXCELLENCE

www.harbourresources.com

THANK YOU

Thank you for taking the time to read *Power Principles: 12 Great Affirmations for Leaders*. The reality is, this wasn't just written so you can read it. It was written to inspire you and ignite purposeful action in your life and leadership.

I urge you to act on these principles, starting today – not next week, next month, or next year, but today. They are time-tested principles, and they work.

As you read, was there something that triggered a thought of a change you need to make? Did a flash of a vision come to mind? Were you reminded of something you always wanted to do and haven't done yet? Were you convicted about making a change to become a better leader?

Now is the time to start.

Whatever your leadership role, be the best you can be – for the sake of those you serve, and for the sake of your own legacy.

If you need a guide, a navigator, or a fellow leader to come alongside you and help you plan and experience Fully Ignited Leadership for yourself or your team, contact me. Helping you lead with passion and excellence is my passion!

ABOUT THE AUTHOR

Mike Harbour is the Founder and President of Harbour Resources in Little Rock, Arkansas. He is a husband of 22-plus years, a father of two amazing children, an avid college football fan (Woo Pig Sooie), a whitetail deer hunter, an average golfer, a U.S. Army Veteran and a lover of leadership and people who desire to become better leaders.

Mike is a Founding Partner of the John Maxwell Team and a select member of the John Maxwell President's Advisory Council.

Mike has helped hire hundreds of leaders and has trained, coached, and spoken to thousands more.

He has won many awards for his leadership, excellence, and speaking...but who cares?

What he wants to know is how can he serve you? How can he help you grow? How can he help you lead at a higher level and build a high-performance team?

For additional resources, visit www.harbourresources.com .